This book is your introduction to a basic vocabulary of more than 500 words in English, French, German and Spanish. It is full of brightly illustrated scenes showing everyday situations that you will instantly recognise.

All the key objects from each scene are individually illustrated and clearly labelled in English, French, German and Spanish. Check the flags to make sure you always recognise the right language!

As you read through the book you will see everything exactly where you would expect to find it and so you will easily learn to read and recognise all the words in each language.

Direct association between scenes, objects and words will also help you to remember them.

Good luck!  Bonne chance!  Viel Glück!  ¡Suerte!

ISBN 1 85854 148 4
© Brimax Books Ltd 1994. All rights reserved.
Published by Brimax Books Ltd, Newmarket, England 1994.
Printed in Spain.

# My First European Dictionary

## Illustrated by Stephanie Ryder

English

French

German

Spanish

BRIMAX • NEWMARKET • ENGLAND

# Useful Words and Phrases

| 🇬🇧 | 🇫🇷 | 🇩🇪 | 🇪🇸 |
|---|---|---|---|
| hello | bonjour | Guten Tag | ¡hola! |
| goodbye | au revoir | Auf Wiedersehen | ¡adios! |
| please | s'il te plaît | bitte | por favor |
| thank you | merci | danke | gracias |
| yes | oui | ja | sí |
| no | non | nein | no |
| morning | le matin | der Morgen | la mañana |
| afternoon | l'après-midi | der Nachmittag | la tarde |
| night | la nuit | die Nacht | la noche |
| excuse me | excuses-moi | Entschuldigung | con permiso |
| tomorrow | demain | morgen | mañana |
| yesterday | hier | gestern | ayer |
| me | moi | mich | me |
| you | tu | du | tú |
| right | à droite | rechts | a la derecha |
| left | à gauche | links | a la izquierda |
| pardon? | pardon? | Wie bitte? | ¿perdón? |

|  |  |  | |
|---|---|---|---|
| What is your name? | Comment t'appelles-tu? | Wie heißt du? | ¿Còmo te llamas? |
| My name is ........................ | Je m'appelle ........................ | Ich heiße ........................ | Me llamo ........................ |
| Where do you live? | Où habites-tu? | Wo wohnst du? | ¿Dónde vives? |
| I live in ........................ | J'habite à ........................ | Ich wohne in ........................ | Vivo en ........................ |
| What time is it? | Quelle heure est-il? | Wie spät ist es? | ¿Qué hora es? |
| I am lost | Je me suis perdu | Ich habe mich verirrt | Me he perdido |
| Good morning | Bonjour | Guten Morgen | Buenos días |
| Good afternoon | Bon aprés-midi | Guten Tag | Buenas tardes |
| Where is the toilet? | Où sont les toilettes? | Wo ist die Toilette? | ¿Dónde está el servicio? |
| How do I get there? | Comment puis-je y aller? | Wie komme ich dorthin? | ¿Cómo voy hasta allí? |

# Numbers

1

2

3

4

5

6

7

8

9

10

| 🇬🇧 | 🇫🇷 | 🇩🇪 | 🇪🇸 |
|---|---|---|---|
| one | un | eins | uno |
| two | deux | zwei | dos |
| three | trois | drei | tres |
| four | quatre | vier | cuatro |
| five | cinq | fünf | cinco |
| six | six | sechs | seis |
| seven | sept | sieben | siete |
| eight | huit | acht | ocho |
| nine | neuf | neun | nueve |
| ten | dix | zehn | diez |

# Numbers

11
12
13
14
15
16
17
18
19
20

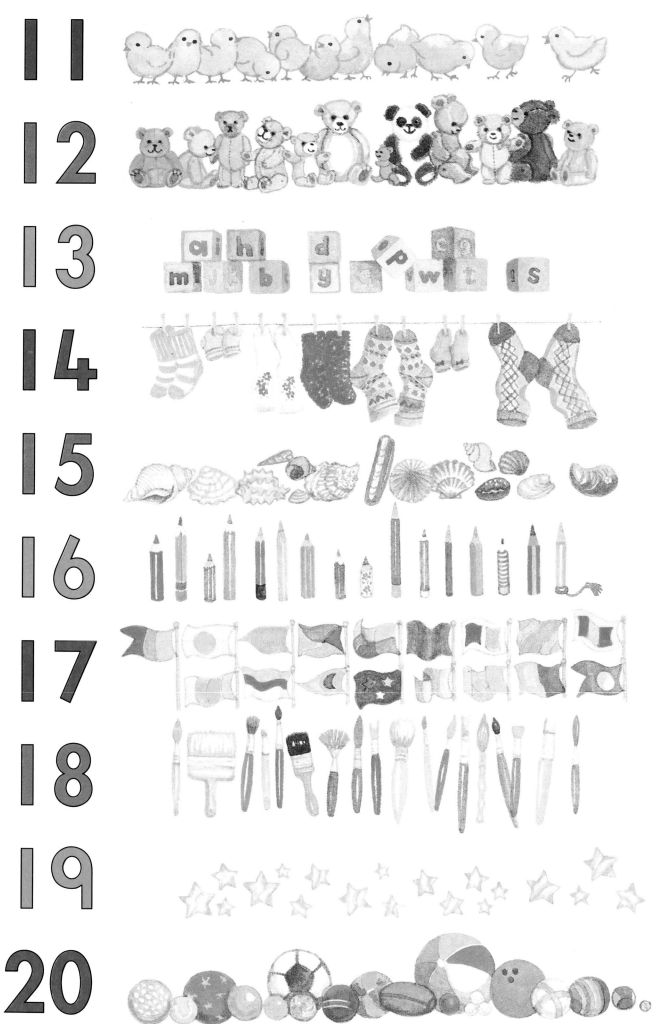

| 🇬🇧 | 🇫🇷 | 🇩🇪 | 🇦🇹 |
|---|---|---|---|
| eleven | onze | elf | once |
| twelve | douze | zwölf | doce |
| thirteen | treize | dreizehn | trece |
| fourteen | quatorze | vierzehn | catorce |
| fifteen | quinze | fünfzehn | quince |
| sixteen | seize | sechzehn | dieciséis |
| seventeen | dix-sept | siebzehn | diecisiete |
| eighteen | dix-huit | achtzehn | dieciocho |
| nineteen | dix-neuf | neunzehn | diecinueve |
| twenty | vingt | zwanzig | veinte |

# Shapes

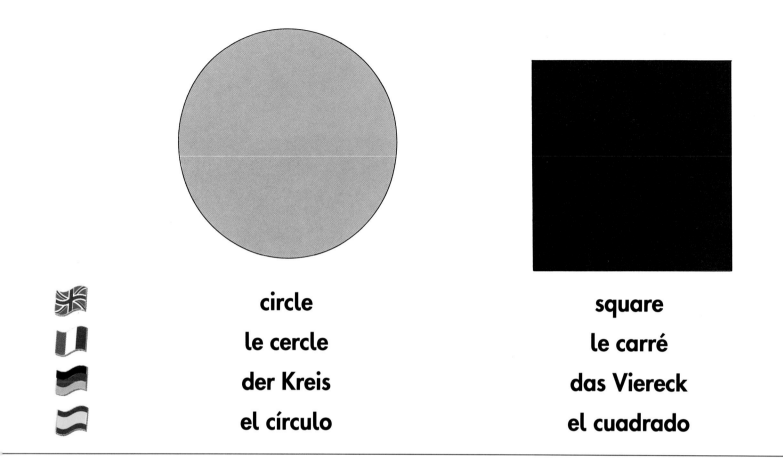

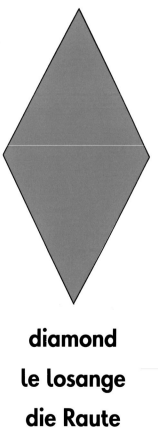

| | circle | | square |
|---|---|---|---|
| | le cercle | | le carré |
| | der Kreis | | das Viereck |
| | el círculo | | el cuadrado |

| | diamond | | star |
|---|---|---|---|
| | le losange | | l'étoile |
| | die Raute | | der Stern |
| | el rombo | | la estrella |

**triangle**

le triangle

das Dreieck

el triángulo

**cross**

la croix

das Kreuz

la cruz

**rectangle**

le rectangle

das Rechteck

el rectángulo

**heart**

le coeur

das Herz

el corazón

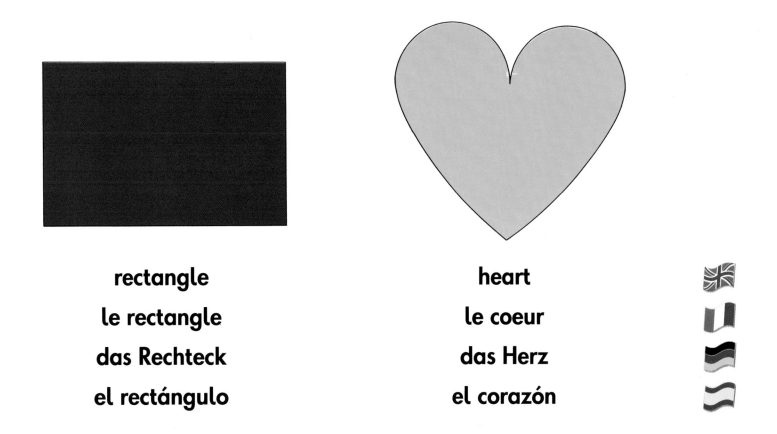

# Parts of the body

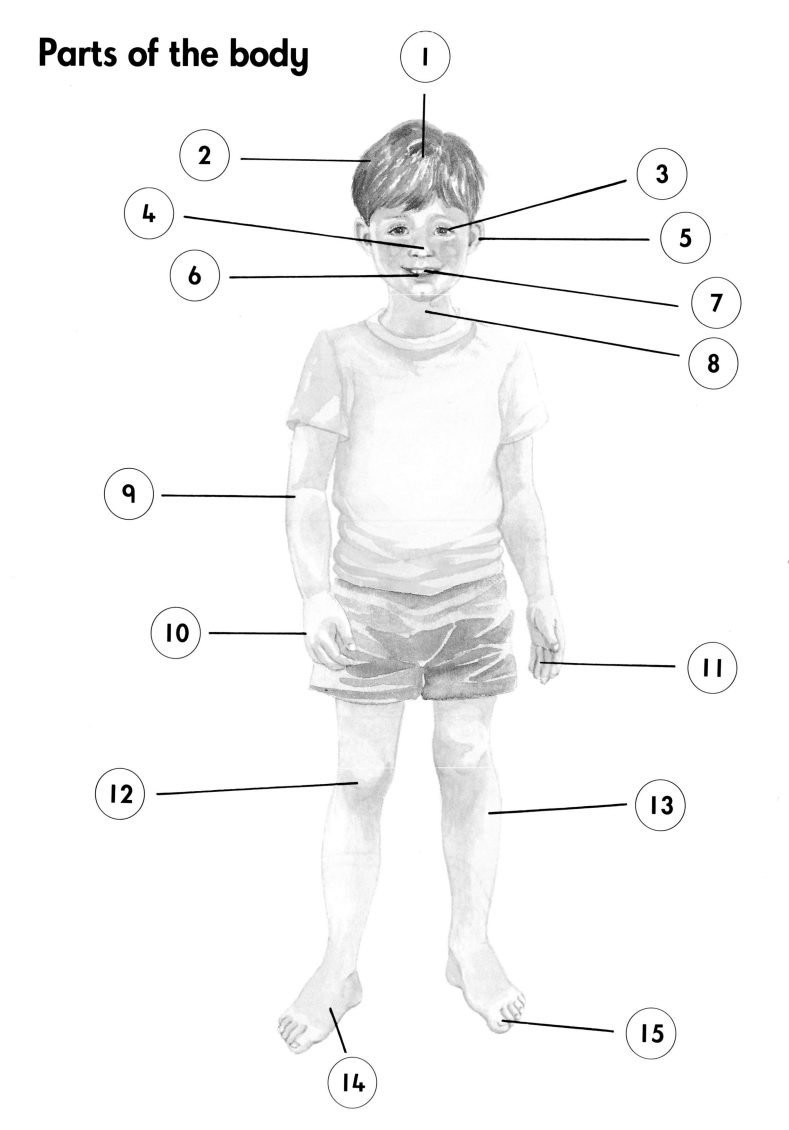

|  | 🇬🇧 | 🇫🇷 | 🇩🇪 | 🇦🇹 |
|---|---|---|---|---|
| 1 | head | la tête | der Kopf | la cabeza |
| 2 | hair | les cheveux | das Haar | el pelo |
| 3 | eye | l'oeil | das Auge | el ojo |
| 4 | nose | le nez | die Nase | la nariz |
| 5 | ear | l'oreille | das Ohr | la oreja |
| 6 | mouth | la bouche | der Mund | la boca |
| 7 | teeth | les dents | die Zähne | los dientes |
| 8 | neck | le cou | der Hals | el cuello |
| 9 | arm | le bras | der Arm | el brazo |
| 10 | hand | la main | die Hand | la mano |
| 11 | fingers | les doigts | die Finger | los dedos |
| 12 | knee | le genou | das Knie | la rodilla |
| 13 | leg | la jambe | das Bein | la pierna |
| 14 | foot | le pied | der Fuß | el pie |
| 15 | toes | les doigts de pied | die Zehen | los dedos del pie |

# Colours

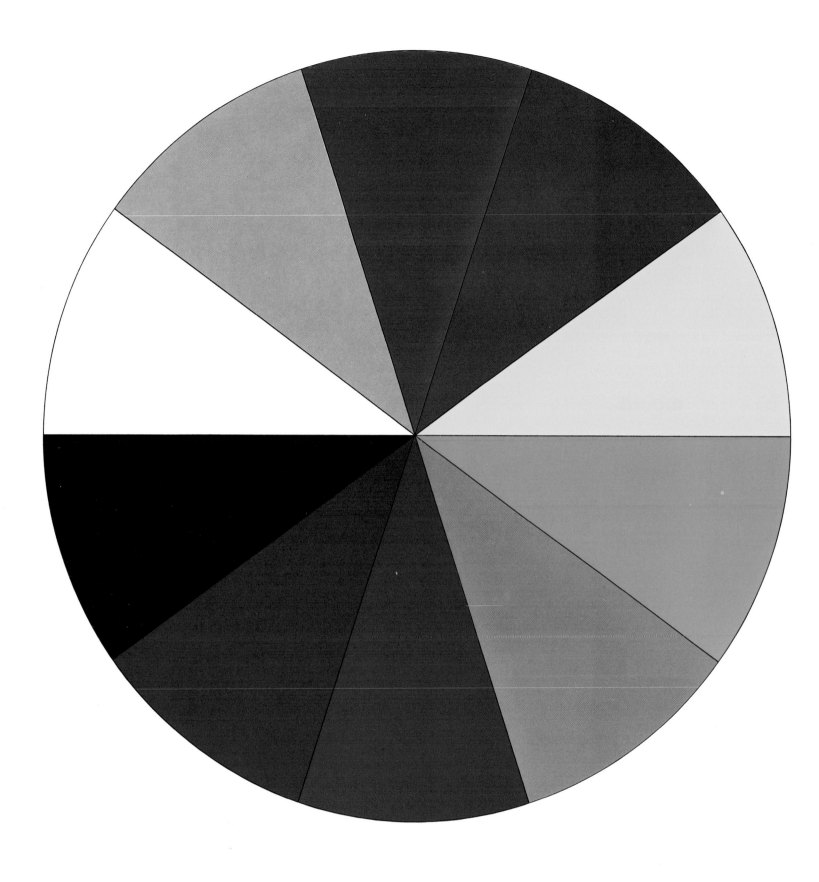

| | | | |
|---|---|---|---|
| red | rouge | rot | rojo |
| blue | bleu | blau | azul |
| yellow | jaune | gelb | amarillo |
| green | vert | grün | verde |
| orange | orange | orange | naranja |
| brown | marron | braun | marrón |
| purple | violet | violett | morado |
| black | noir | schwarz | negro |
| white | blanc | weiß | blanco |
| pink | rose | rosa | rosa |

# Days

| Monday | lundi | Montag | lunes |
| Tuesday | mardi | Dienstag | martes |
| Wednesday | mercredi | Mittwoch | miércoles |
| Thursday | jeudi | Donnerstag | jueves |
| Friday | vendredi | Freitag | viernes |
| Saturday | samedi | Samstag | sábado |
| Sunday | dimanche | Sonntag | domingo |

# Months

| | | | |
|---|---|---|---|
| January | janvier | Januar | enero |
| February | février | Februar | febrero |
| March | mars | März | marzo |
| April | avril | April | abril |
| May | mai | Mai | mayo |
| June | juin | Juni | junio |
| July | juillet | Juli | julio |
| August | août | August | agosto |
| September | septembre | September | septiembre |
| October | octobre | Oktober | octubre |
| November | novembre | November | noviembre |
| December | décembre | Dezember | diciembre |

# Seasons

🇬🇧 **Spring**

🇫🇷 **le printemps**

🇩🇪 **der Frühling**

🇪🇸 **la primavera**

🇬🇧 **Winter**

🇫🇷 **l'hiver**

🇩🇪 **der Winter**

🇪🇸 **el invierno**

Summer

l'été

der Sommer

el verano

Autumn

l'automne

der Herbst

el otoño

# Pets

🇬🇧 pony
🇫🇷 le poney
🇩🇪 das Pony
🇪🇸 el poney

🇬🇧 canary
🇫🇷 le canari
🇩🇪 der Kanarienvogel
🇪🇸 el canario

hamster
le hamster
der Hamster
el hámster

mice
les souris
die Mäuse
los ratones

**dog**

le chien

der Hund

el perro

**cat**

le chat

die Katze

el gato

**guinea pig**

le cochon d'Inde

das Meerschweinchen

el conejillo de Indias

**goldfish**

le poisson rouge

der Goldfisch

el pez de colores

**tortoise**

la tortue

die Schildkröte

la tortuga

**rabbit**

le lapin

das Kaninchen

el conejo

# Opposites

| | 🇬🇧 | 🇫🇷 | 🇩🇪 | 🇦🇹 |
|---|---|---|---|---|
| | big | gros | groß | grande |
| | inside | dedans | drinnen | dentro |
| | happy | gai | fröhlich | contento |
| | hot | chaud | heiß | caliente |
| | wet | mouillé | naß | mojado |
| | fast | rapide | schnell | rápido |
| | up | en haut | hinauf | arriba |
| | over | sur | über | encima |
| | day | le jour | der Tag | el día |
| | hard | dur | hart | duro |

| | 🇬🇧 | 🇫🇷 | 🇩🇪 | 🇪🇸 |
|---|---|---|---|---|
| | small | petit | klein | pequeño |
| | outside | dehors | draußen | fuera |
| | sad | triste | traurig | triste |
| | cold | froid | kalt | frío |
| | dry | sec | trocken | seco |
| | slow | lent | langsam | lento |
| | down | en bas | hinunter | abajo |
| | under | sous | unter | debajo |
| | night | la nuit | die Nacht | la noche |
| | soft | mou | weich | blando |

# Time to get dressed

| | | |
|---|---|---|
| **cap** | **scarf** | **button** |
| la casquette | l'écharpe | le bouton |
| die Mütze | der Schal | der Knopf |
| la visera | la bufanda | el botón |

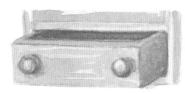

| | | |
|---|---|---|
| **drawer** | **ribbon** | **zipper** |
| le tiroir | le ruban | la fermeture éclair |
| die Schublade | das Band | der Reißverschluß |
| el cajón | la cinta | la cremallera |

| | | |
|---|---|---|
| **shelf** | **hook** | **hanger** |
| l'étagère | le crochet | le cintre |
| das Fach | der Haken | der Kleiderbügel |
| el estante | el perchero | la percha |

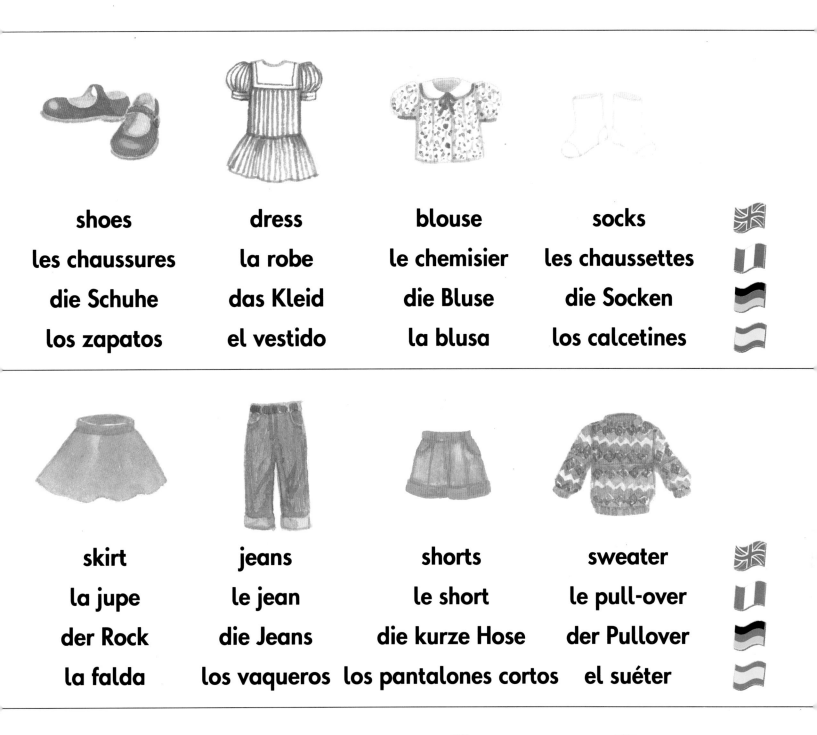

| shoes | dress | blouse | socks |
|---|---|---|---|
| les chaussures | la robe | le chemisier | les chaussettes |
| die Schuhe | das Kleid | die Bluse | die Socken |
| los zapatos | el vestido | la blusa | los calcetines |

| skirt | jeans | shorts | sweater |
|---|---|---|---|
| la jupe | le jean | le short | le pull-over |
| der Rock | die Jeans | die kurze Hose | der Pullover |
| la falda | los vaqueros | los pantalones cortos | el suéter |

| t-shirt | jacket | trousers | coat |
|---|---|---|---|
| le tee-shirt | la veste | le pantalon | le manteau |
| das T-Shirt | die Jacke | die Hose | der Mantel |
| la camiseta | la chaqueta | los pantalones | el abrigo |

# Can you say these words in French, German and Spanish?

shoes

dress

blouse

socks

cap

skirt

jeans

coat

sweater

t-shirt

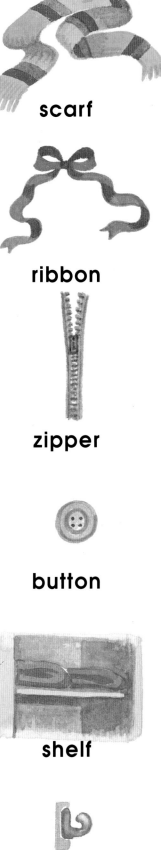

scarf

ribbon

zipper

button

shelf

hook

jacket

trousers

shorts

drawer

hanger

# Learn and play

dinosaur
le dinosaure
der Dinosaurier
el dinosaurio

apron
le tablier
die Schürze
el delantal

fingerpaint
la peinture avec les doigts
die Fingerfarbe
la pintura con dedos

paint brush
le pinceau
der Pinsel
el pincel

chalk
la craie
die Kreide
la tiza

paper
le papier
das Papier
el papel

scissors
la paire de ciseaux
die Schere
las tijeras

pencil
le crayon
der Bleistift
el lápiz

| picture | desk | blackboard |  |
| le dessin | le bureau | le tableau noir | |
| das Bild | der Schreibtisch | die Tafel | |
| el dibujo | el pupitre | la pizarra | |

| sandbox | cloth | crayon |  |
| la bac à sable | le chiffon | le crayon | |
| der Sandkasten | das Tuch | der Wachsstift | |
| el cajón de arena | el trapo | el lápiz de cera | |

| clock | glue | paint |
| la pendule | la colle | la peinture |
| die Uhr | der Leim | die Farbe |
| el reloj | la cola | la pintura |

# Can you say these words in French, German and Spanish?

paint brush

picture

scissors

paint

pencil

chalk

blackboard

clock

apron

cloth

sandbox

glue

dinosaur

fingerpaint

desk

crayon

paper

# At the beach

starfish
l'étoile de mer
der Seestern
la estrella de mar

towel
la serviette
das Badetuch
la toalla

bucket
le seau
der Eimer
el cubo

flag
le drapeau
die Fahne
la bandera

sand
le sable
der Sand
la arena

ship
le bateau
das Schiff
el barco

seagull
la mouette
die Möwe
la gaviota

crab
la crabe
die Krabbe
el cangrejo

**shell**

le coquillage

die Muschel

la concha de mar

**sandcastle**

le château de sable

die Sandburg

el castillo de arena

**lighthouse**

le phare

der Leuchtturm

el faro

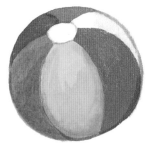

**beachball**

le ballon

der Wasserball

el balón

**hat**

le chapeau

der Hut

el sombrero

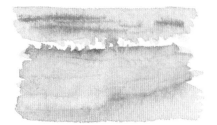

**sea**

la mer

das Meer

el mar

**ice-cream**

la glace

das Eis

el helado

**rock**

le rocher

der Fels

la roca

**bucket**

Can you say these words in French, German and Spanish?

**flag**

**beachball**

**ship**

**towel**

**sandcastle**

**seagull**

**starfish**

**ice-cream**

**rock**

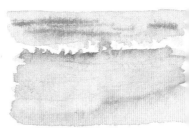

**sea**

**hat**

**crab**

**shell**

**lighthouse**

**sand**

# Shopping

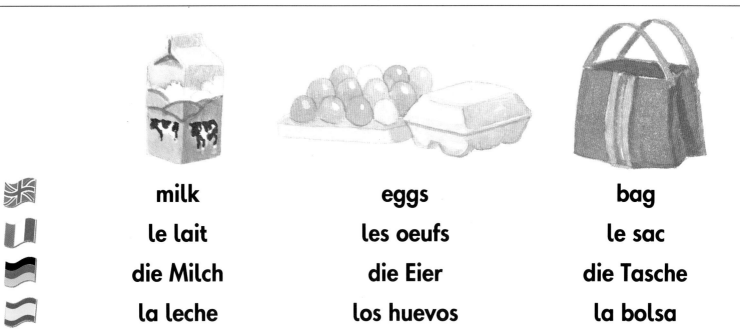

 milk  
le lait  
die Milch  
la leche

eggs  
les oeufs  
die Eier  
los huevos

bag  
le sac  
die Tasche  
la bolsa

bread  
le pain  
das Brot  
el pan

cheese  
le fromage  
der Käse  
el queso

potatoes  
les pommes de terre  
die Kartoffeln  
las patatas

oranges  
les oranges  
die Orangen  
las naranjas

apples  
les pommes  
die Äpfel  
las manzanas

meat  
la viande  
das Fleisch  
la carne

**grapes**
les raisins
die Trauben
las uvas

**sausages**
les saucisses
die Würste
las salchichas

**tomatoes**
les tomates
die Tomaten
los tomates

**basket**
le panier
der Korb
la cesta

**carrots**
les carottes
die Karotten
las zanahorias

**purse**
le porte-monnaie
der Geldbeutel
el monedero

**money**
l'argent
das Geld
el dinero

**bananas**
les bananes
die Bananen
los plátanos

**chocolate**
le chocolat
die Schokolade
el chocolate

# Can you say these words in French, German and Spanish?

bread

eggs

cheese

milk

potatoes

oranges

apples

meat

grapes

sausages

tomatoes

basket

purse

money

bag

carrots

chocolate

bananas

# The doctor's office

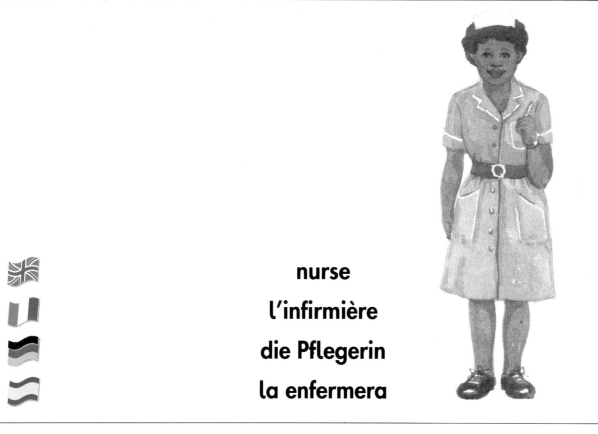

nurse

l'infirmière

die Pflegerin

la enfermera

wheelchair

le fauteuil roulant

der Rollstuhl

la silla de ruedas

scissors

les ciseaux

die Schere

las tijeras

Band-Aid™

le sparadrap

das Pflaster

la tirita

bandage

le pansement

die Binde

la venda

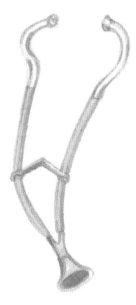

**stethoscope**

le stéthoscope

das Stethoskop

el estetoscopio

**thermometer**

le thermomètre

das Thermometer

el termómetro

**doctor**

le médecin

der Arzt

el médico

**medicine**

le médicament

die Medizin

la medicina

**cream**

la pommade

die Salbe

la pomada

**spoon**

la cuillère

der Löffel

la cuchara

**doctor**

**nurse**

**spoon**

**thermometer**

Can you say these words in French, German and Spanish?

**Band-Aid** ™

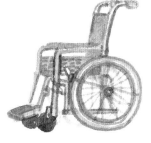
**wheelchair**

**stethoscope**

**scissors**

**medicine**

**bandage**

**cream**

# In the garden

| 🇬🇧 | wheel barrow | flower pot | watering can |
| 🇫🇷 | la brouette | le pot de fleur | l'arrosoir |
| 🇩🇪 | die Schubkarre | der Blumentopf | die Gießkanne |
| 🇪🇸 | la carretilla | el tiesto | la regadera |

| 🇬🇧 | trees | sprinkler | bush |
| 🇫🇷 | les arbres | l'arroseur à jet tournant | le buisson |
| 🇩🇪 | die Bäume | der Rasensprenger | der Busch |
| 🇪🇸 | los árboles | el aspersor | el arbusto |

| 🇬🇧 | grass | hose | pond |
| 🇫🇷 | l'herbe | le tuyau d'arrosage | l'étang |
| 🇩🇪 | das Gras | der Schlauch | der Teich |
| 🇪🇸 | la hierba | la manguera | el estanque |

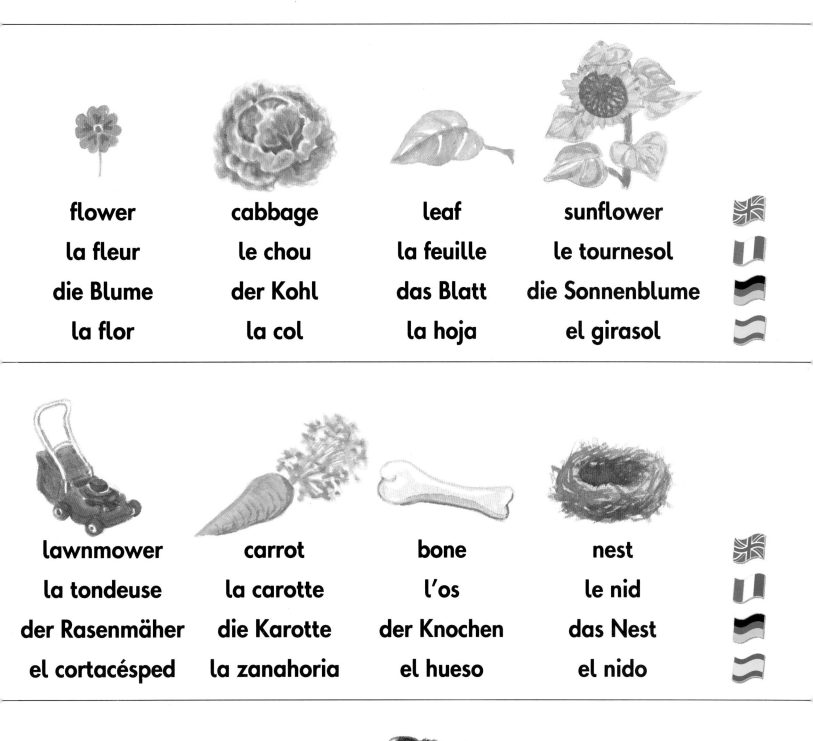

| flower | cabbage | leaf | sunflower |
|--------|---------|------|-----------|
| la fleur | le chou | la feuille | le tournesol |
| die Blume | der Kohl | das Blatt | die Sonnenblume |
| la flor | la col | la hoja | el girasol |

| lawnmower | carrot | bone | nest |
|-----------|--------|------|------|
| la tondeuse | la carotte | l'os | le nid |
| der Rasenmäher | die Karotte | der Knochen | das Nest |
| el cortacésped | la zanahoria | el hueso | el nido |

| ant | cat | dog | bird |
|-----|-----|-----|------|
| la fourmi | le chat | le chien | l'oiseau |
| die Ameise | die Katze | der Hund | der Vogel |
| la hormiga | el gato | el perro | el pájaro |

# Can you say these words in French, German and Spanish?

watering can

flower

hose

cabbage

sprinkler

flower pot

wheel barrow

lawnmower

cat

grass

trees

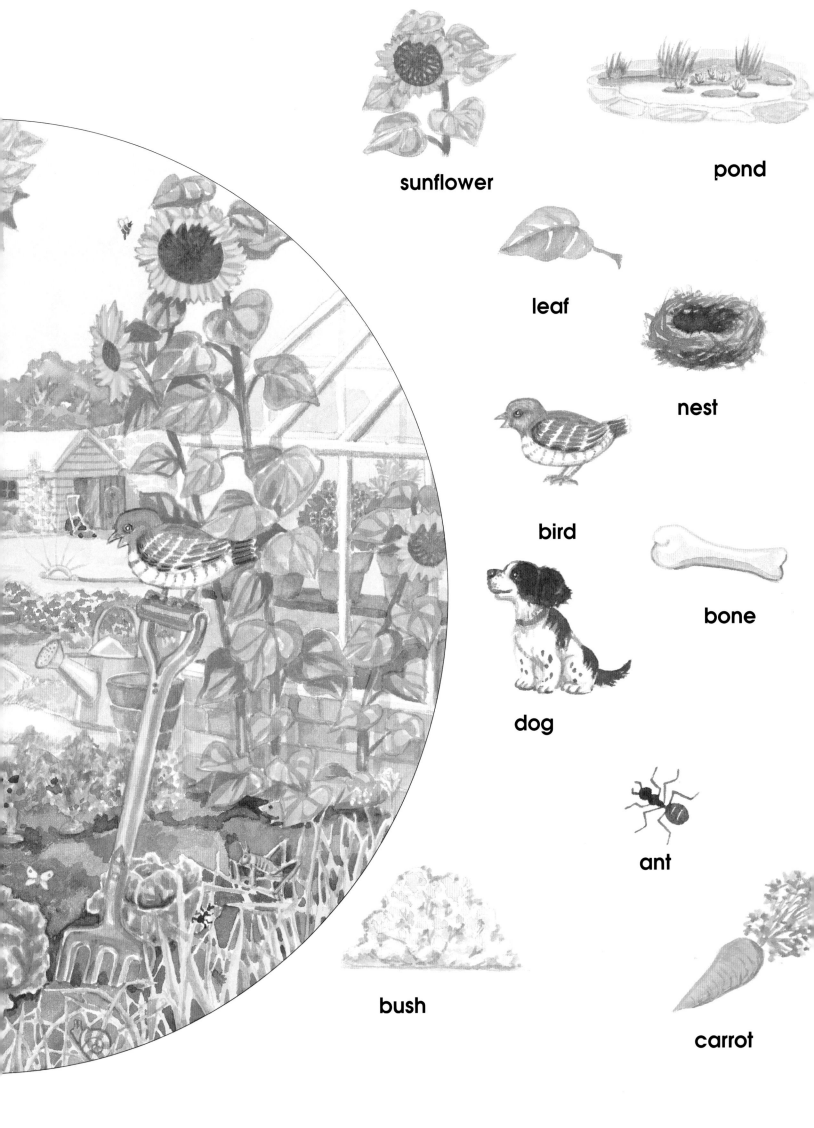

sunflower

pond

leaf

nest

bird

bone

dog

ant

bush

carrot

# Toy store

🇬🇧 jack-in-the-box
🇫🇷 le diable à ressort
🇩🇪 der Schachtelkasperl
🇪🇸 la caja sorpresa

jig-saw puzzle
le puzzle
das Puzzlespiel
el puzzle

🇬🇧 truck
🇫🇷 le camion
🇩🇪 der Lastwagen
🇪🇸 el camión

helicopter
l'hélicoptère
der Hubschrauber
el helicóptero

plane
l'avion
das Flugzeug
el avión

🇬🇧 car
🇫🇷 la voiture
🇩🇪 das Auto
🇪🇸 el coche

tunnel
le tunnel
der Tunnel
el túnel

train
le train
die Lokomotive
el tren

track
la voie
das Gleis
la vía

**teddy bear**

l'ours en peluche

der Teddybär

el osito de peluche

**rocking-horse**

le cheval à bascule

das Schaukelpferd

el caballo de balancín

**doll**

la poupée

die Puppe

la muñeca

**clown**

le clown

der Clown

el payaso

**drum**

le tambour

die Trommel

el tambor

**book**

le livre

das Buch

el libro

**blocks**

les cubes

die Bauklötze

los cubos

**trumpet**

la trompette

die Trompete

la trompeta

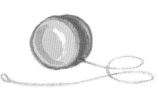

**yo-yo**

le yo-yo

das Yo-Yo

el yo-yo

**ball**

le ballon

der Ball

el balón

**jack-in the-box**

**doll**

**teddy bear**

**train**

**jig-saw puzzle**

Can you say these words in French, German and Spanish?

**car**

**drum**

**book**

**plane**

rocking
horse

truck

ball

yo-yo

track

blocks   clown

trumpet   helicopter

tunnel

# A rainy day

**cloud**
le nuage
die Wolke
la nube

**bridge**
le pont
die Brücke
el puente

**fence**
la palissade
der Zaun
la valla

**train**
le train
der Zug
el tren

**boots**
les bottes
die Gummistiefel
las botas

**rain hat**
le chapeau de pluie
die Regenhaube
el gorro de lluvia

**puddle**
la flaque d'eau
die Pfütze
el charco

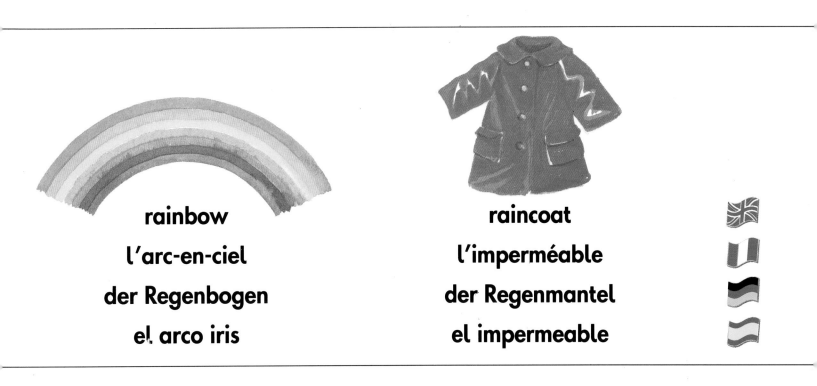

**rainbow**

l'arc-en-ciel

der Regenbogen

el arco iris

**raincoat**

l'imperméable

der Regenmantel

el impermeable

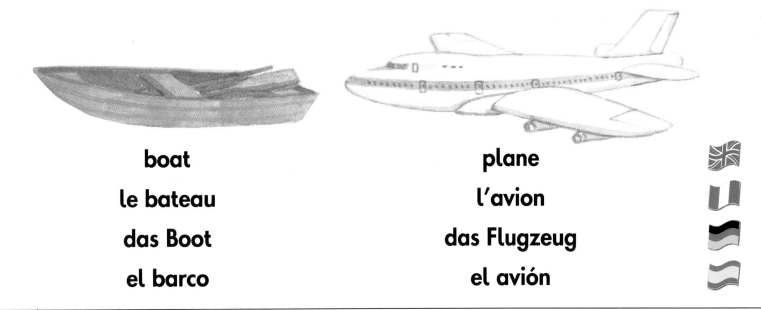

**boat**

le bateau

das Boot

el barco

**plane**

l'avion

das Flugzeug

el avión

**umbrella**

le parapluie

der Schirm

el paraguas

**frog**

la grenouille

der Frosch

la rana

**wheel**

la roue

das Rad

la rueda

**wall**

le mur

die Mauer

el muro

# Can you say these words in French, German and Spanish?

puddle

boots

rainbow

frog

bridge

boat

cloud

umbrella

wheel

fence

wall

tent

train

plane

raincoat

rain hat

# On the farm

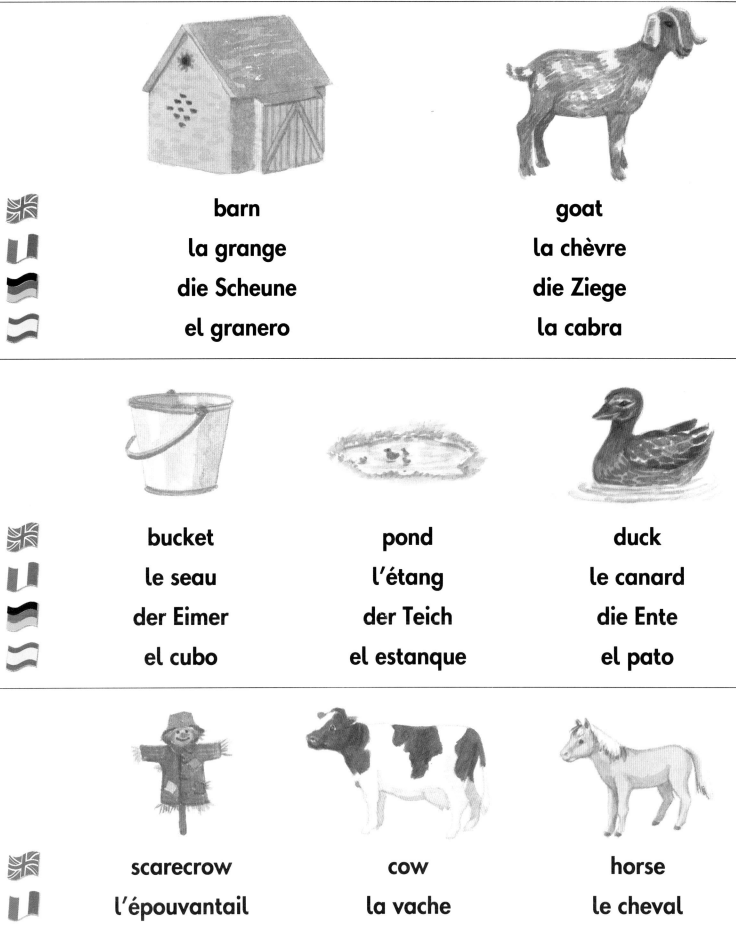

**barn**
la grange
die Scheune
el granero

**goat**
la chèvre
die Ziege
la cabra

**bucket**
le seau
der Eimer
el cubo

**pond**
l'étang
der Teich
el estanque

**duck**
le canard
die Ente
el pato

**scarecrow**
l'épouvantail
die Vogelscheuche
el espantapájaros

**cow**
la vache
die Kuh
la vaca

**horse**
le cheval
das Pferd
el caballo

**lamb**

l'agneau

das Lamm

el cordero

**turkey**

le dindon

der Truthahn

el pavo

**goose**

l'oie

die Gans

la oca

**pig**

le cochon

das Schwein

el cerdo

**chick**

le poussin

das Küken

el pollito

**feathers**

les plumes

die Federn

las plumas

**tractor**

le tracteur

der Traktor

el tractor

**farmer**

le fermier

der Bauer

el granjero

**stable**

l'écurie

der Stall

la caballeriza

**tractor**

**pig**

**chick**

**goat**

Can you say these words in French, German and Spanish?

**lamb**

**duck**

**horse**         **scarecrow**     **cow**

**feathers**

**bucket**

**turkey**

**goose**

**pond**

**farmer**

**stable**

**barn**

# In the snow

🇬🇧 **ice skates**
🇫🇷 **les patins à glace**
🇩🇪 **die Schlittschuhe**
🇪🇸 **los patines de cuchilla**

**snowflake**
**le flocon de neige**
**die Schneeflocke**
**el copo de nieve**

**icicles**
**les glaçons**
**die Eiszapfen**
**los carám banos**

🇬🇧 **toboggan**
🇫🇷 **la luge**
🇩🇪 **der Rodelschlitten**
🇪🇸 **el trineo**

**snowman**
**le bonhomme de neige**
**der Schneemann**
**el muñeco de nieve**

**skis**
**les skis**
**die Skier**
**los esquís**

🇬🇧 **trees**
🇫🇷 **les arbres**
🇩🇪 **die Bäume**
🇪🇸 **los árboles**

**iceberg**
**le glacier**
**der Eisberg**
**el iceberg**

**pipe**
**la pipe**
**die Pfeife**
**la pipa**

**jacket**
**la veste**
**die Jacke**
**la chaqueta**

**mittens**
les moufles
die Fausthandschuhe
las manoplas

**scarf**
l'écharpe
der Schal
la bufanda

**robin**
le rouge-gorge
das Rotkehlchen
el petirrojo

**snowballs**
les boules de neige
die Schneebälle
las bolas de nieve

**mountain**
la montagne
der Berg
la montaña

**gloves**
les gants
die Handschuhe
los guantes

**igloo**
le igloo
der Iglu
el iglú

**eskimo**
l'esquimau
der Eskimo
el esquimal

**hat**
le bonnet
die Mütze
el gorro

**coat**
le manteau
der Mantel
el abrigo

# Can you say these words in French, German and Spanish?

ice skates

snowman

skis

gloves

scarf

mittens

snowballs

icicles

hat

robin

pipe

mountain

coat

jacket

snowflake

iceberg

igloo

eskimo

trees

toboggan

# Working outside

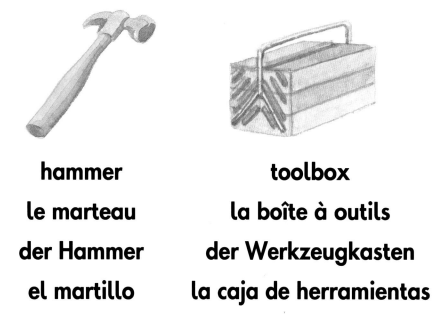

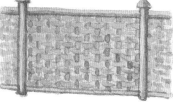

| | | |
|---|---|---|
| **hammer** | **toolbox** | **nail** |
| le marteau | la boîte à outils | le clou |
| der Hammer | der Werkzeugkasten | der Nagel |
| el martillo | la caja de herramientas | el clavo |

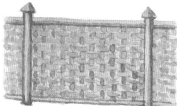

| | | |
|---|---|---|
| **paint** | **fence** | **ladder** |
| la peinture | la palissade | l'échelle |
| die Farbe | der Zaun | die Leiter |
| la pintura | la valla | la escalera de mano |

| | | |
|---|---|---|
| **window** | **garage** | **broom** |
| la fenêtre | le garage | le balai |
| das Fenster | die Garage | der Besen |
| la ventana | el garaje | la escoba |

| | | |
|---|---|---|
| **house** | **chimney** | **path** |
| la maison | la cheminée | le chemin |
| das Haus | der Schornstein | der Weg |
| la casa | la chimenea | el camino |

| | | |
|---|---|---|
| **spider** | **axe** | **car** |
| l'araignée | la hache | la voiture |
| die Spinne | die Axt | das Auto |
| la araña | el hacha | el coche |

| | | |
|---|---|---|
| **roof** | **cobweb** | **door** |
| le toit | la toile d'araignée | la porte |
| das Dach | das Spinnennetz | die Tür |
| el tejado | la telaraña | la puerta |

**hammer**

Can you say these words in French, German and Spanish?

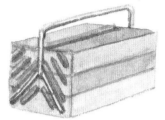

**toolbox**

**nail**

**paint**

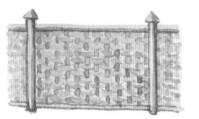

**fence**

**ladder**

**window**

**garage**

**broom**

**cobweb**

**spider**

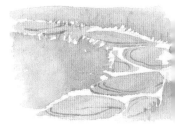

**path**

**chimney**

**axe**

**door**

**car**

**house**

**roof**

# A birthday party

| | | |
|---|---|---|
| | **tablecloth** | **cake** |
| | la nappe | le gâteau |
| | die Tischdecke | die Torte |
| | el mantel | el pastel |

| | | |
|---|---|---|
| | **napkin** | **balloon** | **necklace** |
| | la serviette | le ballon | le collier |
| | die Serviette | der Luftballon | die Kette |
| | la servilleta | el globo | el collar |

| | | |
|---|---|---|
| | **ice-cream** | **telephone** | **straw** |
| | la glace | le téléphone | la paille |
| | das Eis | das Telefon | der Trinkhalm |
| | el helado | el teléfono | la pajita |

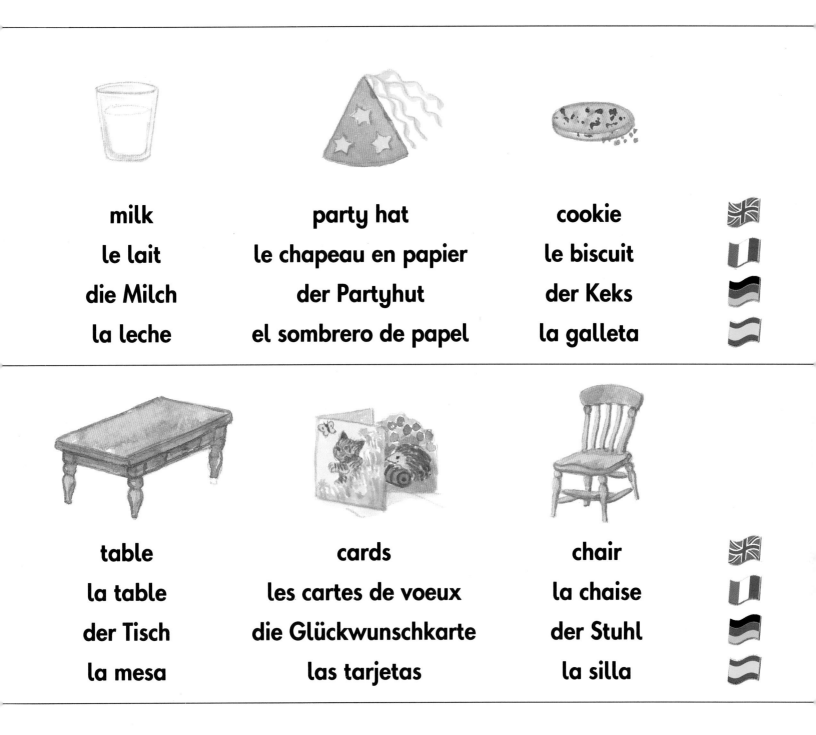

**milk**
le lait
die Milch
la leche

**party hat**
le chapeau en papier
der Partyhut
el sombrero de papel

**cookie**
le biscuit
der Keks
la galleta

**table**
la table
der Tisch
la mesa

**cards**
les cartes de voeux
die Glückwunschkarte
las tarjetas

**chair**
la chaise
der Stuhl
la silla

**candle**
la bougie
die Kerze
la vela

**camera**
l'appareil-photo
der Fotoapparat
la máquina fotográfica

**presents**
les cadeaux
die Geschenke
los regalos

# Can you say these words in French, German and Spanish?

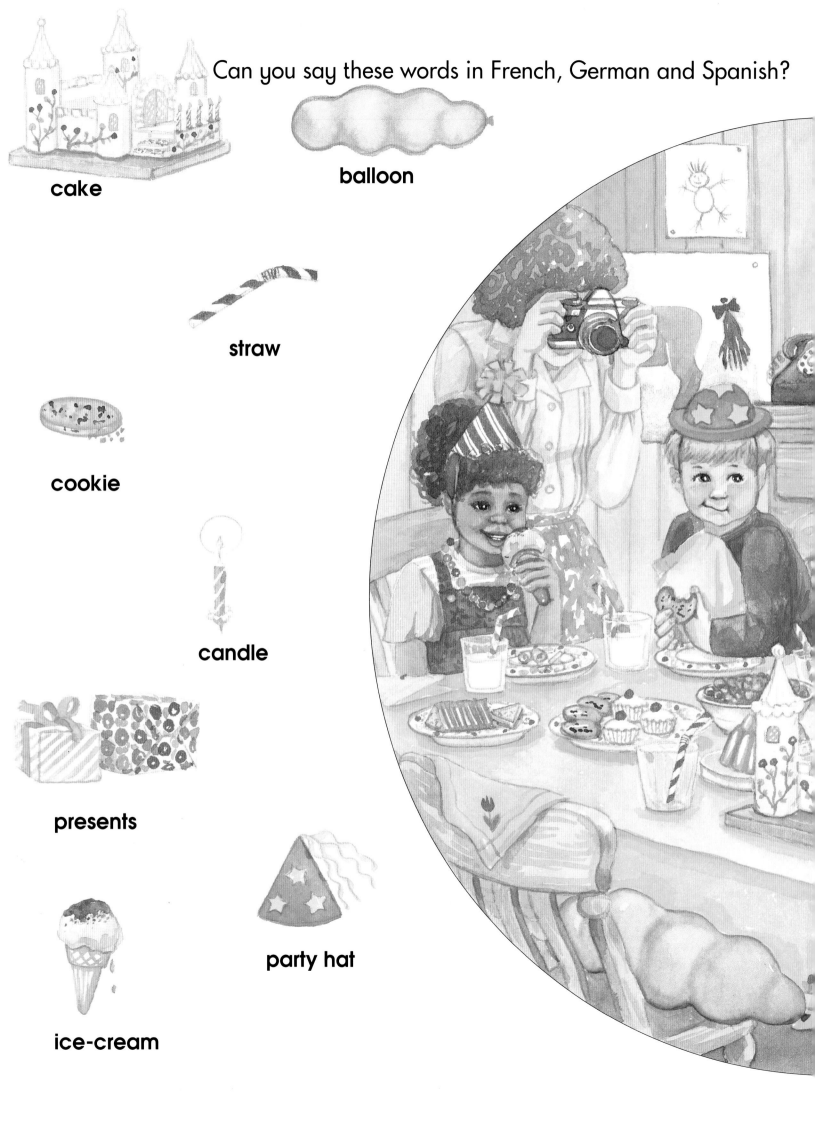

cake

balloon

straw

cookie

candle

presents

party hat

ice-cream

telephone

milk

necklace

cards

camera

napkin

tablecloth

table

chair

# In the kitchen

 **mixing bowl**
 **rolling pin**
 **glass**

le bol     le rouleau à pâtisserie     le verre

die Rührschüssel     das Nudelholz     das Glas

la bol     el rodillo de cocina     el vaso

**butter**     **wooden spoon**     **flour**

le beurre     la cuillère en bois     la farine

die Butter     der Holzlöffel     das Mehl

la mantequilla     la cuchara de madera     la harina

 **knife**     **fork**     **spoon**     **plate**

le couteau     la fourchette     la cuillère     l'assiette

das Messer     die Gabel     der Löffel     der Teller

el cuchillo     el tenedor     la cuchara     el plato

**stove**
la cuisinière
der Herd
la cocina

**microwave**
le four à micro-ondes
der Mikrowellenherd
el microondas

**apron**
le tablier
die Schürze
el delantal

**toaster**
le grille-pain
der Toaster
el tostador

**sink**
l'évier
die Spüle
el fregadero

**saucepan**
la casserole
der Kochtopf
la cacerola

**cup**
la tasse
die Tasse
la taza

**eggs**
les oeufs
die Eier
los huevos

**table**
la table
der Tisch
la mesa

**chair**
la chaise
der Stuhl
la silla

stove

flour

butter

mixing bowl

eggs

Can you say these words in French, German and Spanish?

rolling pin

apron

wooden
spoon

table

plate

**toaster**

**microwave**

**saucepan**

**chair**

**sink**

**cup**

**knife**

**spoon**

**fork**

**glass**

# At the park

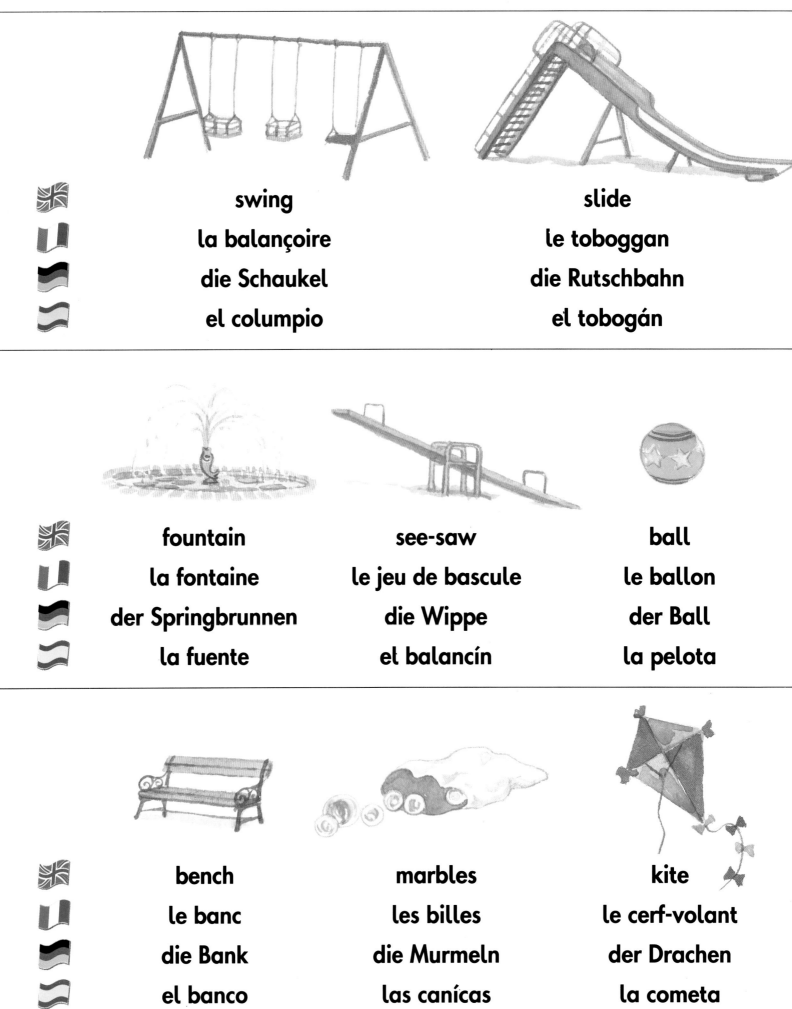

swing
la balançoire
die Schaukel
el columpio

slide
le toboggan
die Rutschbahn
el tobogán

fountain
la fontaine
der Springbrunnen
la fuente

see-saw
le jeu de bascule
die Wippe
el balancín

ball
le ballon
der Ball
la pelota

bench
le banc
die Bank
el banco

marbles
les billes
die Murmeln
las canícas

kite
le cerf-volant
der Drachen
la cometa

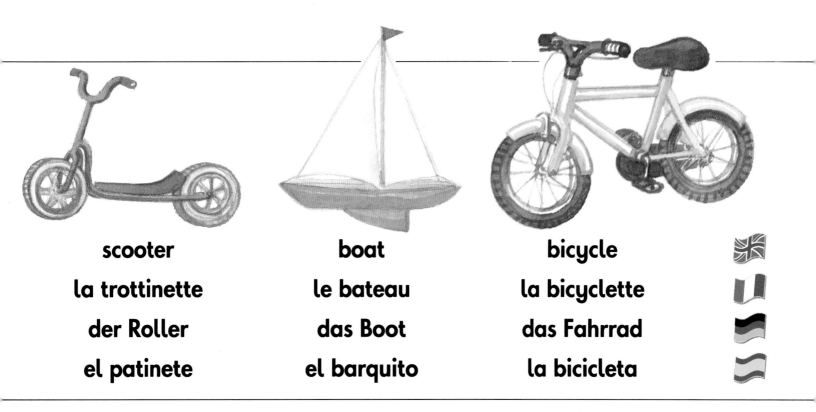

**scooter**

la trottinette

der Roller

el patinete

**boat**

le bateau

das Boot

el barquito

**bicycle**

la bicyclette

das Fahrrad

la bicicleta

**sandbox**

le bac à sable

der Sandkasten

el cajón de arena

**bat**

la batte de baseball

der Schläger

el bate de béisbol

**rollerskates**

les patins à roulettes

die Rollschuhe

los patines de ruedas

**skateboard**

le skateboard

das Skateboard

el monopatín

Can you say these words in French, German and Spanish?

kite

fountain

boat

see-saw

sandbox

swing

slide

bench

scooter

rollerskates

marbles

bicycle

bat

ball

skateboard

# Christmas

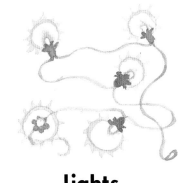

🇬🇧 **Christmas tree**

🇫🇷 l'arbre de Noël

🇩🇪 der Christbaum

🇪🇸 el árbol de Navidad

**tinsel**

la guirlande de Noël

das Lamette

las guirnaldas

🇬🇧 **lights**

🇫🇷 les lampions

🇩🇪 die Lichter

🇪🇸 las luces

**presents**

les cadeaux

die Geschenke

los regalos

**mistletoe**

le gui

der Mistelzweig

el muérdago

🇬🇧 **angel**

🇫🇷 l'ange

🇩🇪 der Engel

🇪🇸 el ángel

**bell**

la cloche

die Glocke

la campanilla

**star**

l'étoile

der Stern

la estrella

**Santa Claus**

le Père Noël

Nikolaus

el Papá Noel

**cards**

les cartes de voeux

die Weihnachtskarten

las tarjetas de Navidad

**stocking**

les chaussettes de Noël

der Strumpf

el calcetín

**holly**

le houx

die Stechpalme

el acebo

**sleigh**

le traîneau

der Schlitten

el trineo

**boots**

les bottes

die Stiefel

las botas

**beard**

la barbe

der Bart

la barba

**belt**

la ceinture

der Gürtel

el cinturón

**lantern**

la lanterne

die Laterne

la linterna

**reindeer**

le renne

das Ren

el reno

**Christmas tree**

**lights**

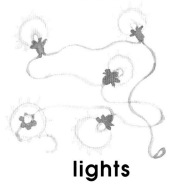

**tinsel**

**cards**

**holly**

**Can you say these words in French, German and Spanish?**

**stocking**

**presents**

**mistletoe**

**angel**

**star**

**bell**

**belt**

**boots**

**beard**

**Santa Claus**

**reindeer**

**sleigh**

**lantern**

# By the river

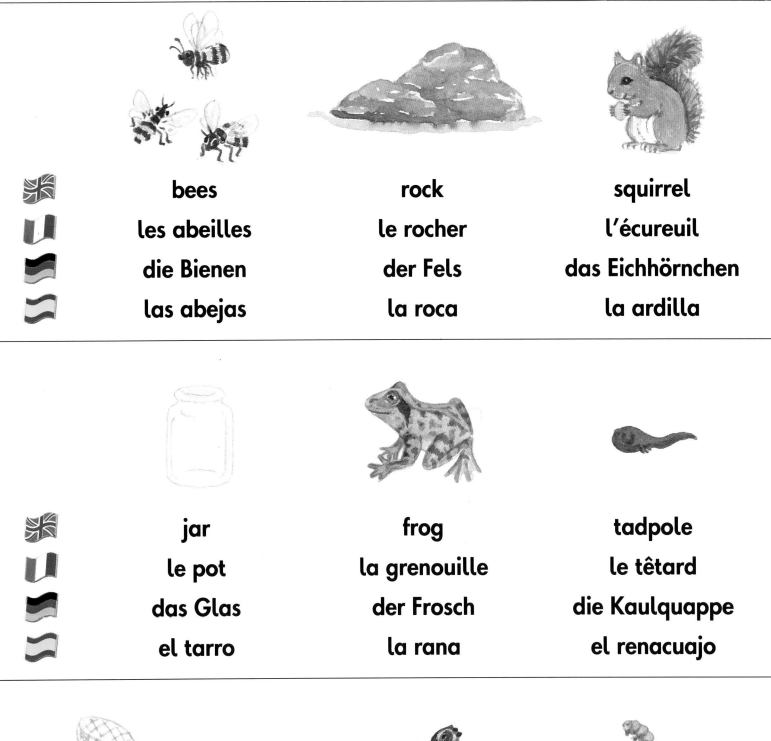

**bees**
les abeilles
die Bienen
las abejas

**rock**
le rocher
der Fels
la roca

**squirrel**
l'écureuil
das Eichhörnchen
la ardilla

**jar**
le pot
das Glas
el tarro

**frog**
la grenouille
der Frosch
la rana

**tadpole**
le têtard
die Kaulquappe
el renacuajo

**net**
le filet
der Kescher
la red

**butterfly**
le papillon
der Schmetterling
la mariposa

**caterpillar**
la chenille
die Raupe
la oruga

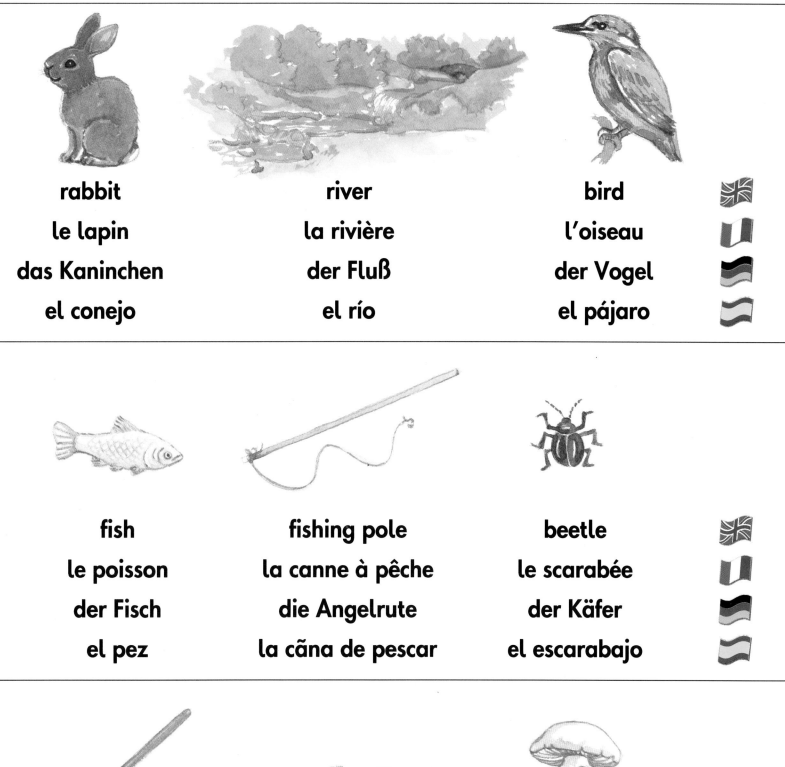

**rabbit**
le lapin
das Kaninchen
el conejo

**river**
la rivière
der Fluß
el río

**bird**
l'oiseau
der Vogel
el pájaro

**fish**
le poisson
der Fisch
el pez

**fishing pole**
la canne à pêche
die Angelrute
la cãna de pescar

**beetle**
le scarabée
der Käfer
el escarabajo

**oar**
la rame
das Ruder
el remo

**rowing boat**
le bateau à rames
das Ruderboot
el bote de remo

**mushroom**
le champignon
der Pilz
el champiñón

**fish**

Can you say these words in French, German and Spanish?

**caterpillar**

**bees**

**jar**     **rabbit**

**tadpole**

**fishing pole**

**net**

**butterfly**

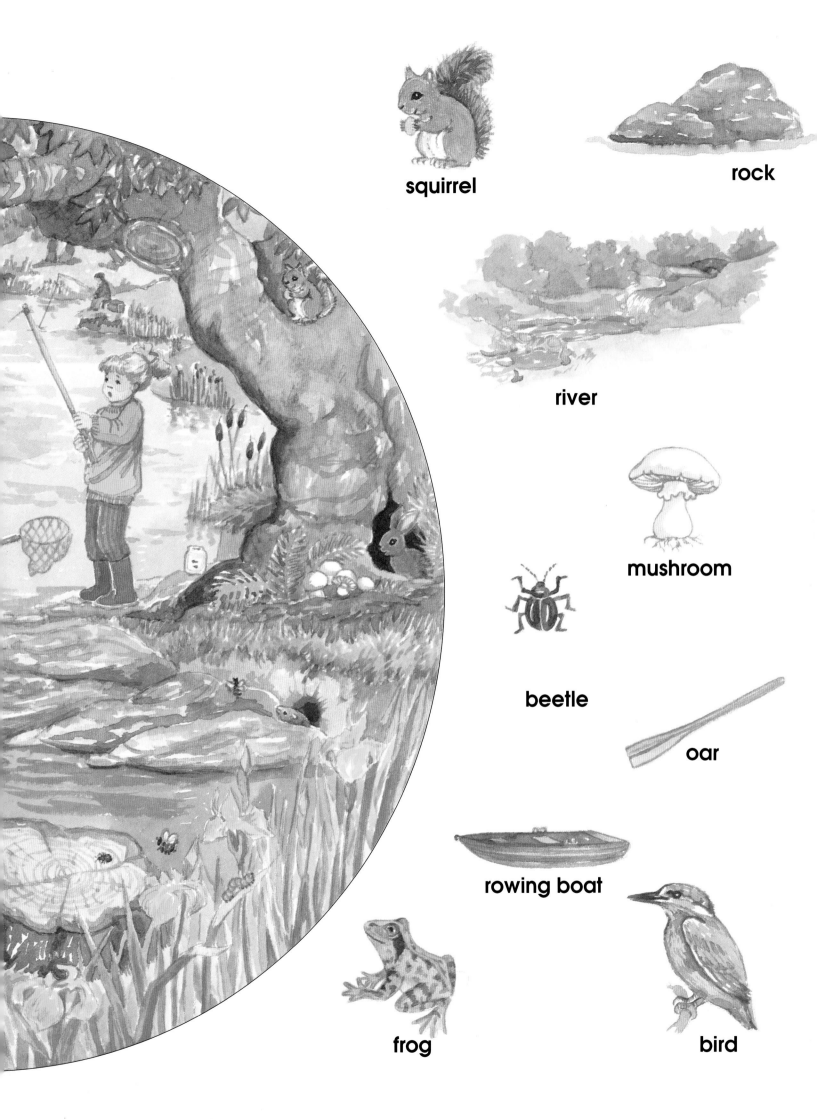

squirrel

rock

river

mushroom

beetle

oar

rowing boat

frog

bird

# Time for bed

 **toybox**
la boîte à jouets
die Spielzeugkasten
la caja de juguetes

**toothbrush**
la brosse à dents
die Zahnbürste
el cepillo de dientes

**mirror**
le miroir
der Spiegel
el espejo

**teddy bear**
l'ours en peluche
der Teddybär
el osito de peluche

**bubbles**
les bulles de savon
die Seifenblasen
las burbujas

**sponge**
l'éponge
der Schwamm
la esponja

**storybook**
le livre d'histoires
das Märchenbuch
el libro de cuentos

**brush**
la brosse à cheveux
die Bürste
el cepillo

**comb**
le peigne
der Kamm
el peine

| | | | |
|---|---|---|---|
| **slippers** | **quilt** | **pillow** | **bed** |
| les pantoufles | l'édredon | l'oreiller | le lit |
| die Hausschuhe | die Bettdecke | das Kopfkissen | das Bett |
| las zapatillas | el edredón | la almohada | la cama |

| | | | |
|---|---|---|---|
| **bath-tub** | **soap** | **towel** | **sheet** |
| la baignoire | le savon | la serviette | le drap |
| die Badewanne | die Seife | das Handtuch | das Laken |
| la bañera | el jabón | la toalla | la sábana |

| | | | |
|---|---|---|---|
| **owl** | **rug** | **moon** | **lamp** |
| le hibou | le tapis | la lune | la lampe |
| die Eule | der Teppich | der Mond | die Lampe |
| el búho | la alfomba | la luna | la lámpara |

stars

slippers

comb

brush

mirror

pillow

## Can you say these words in French, German and Spanish?

bed

bath-tub

toothbrush

soap

sponge

quilt

**toys**

**owl**

**moon**

**rug**

**bubbles**

**toybox**

**storybook**

**teddy bear**

**sheet**

**towel**

**lamp**

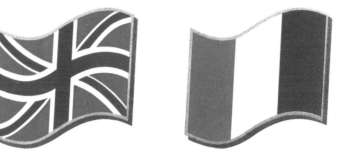